HELP MY UNBELIEF

devotional poems & prayers

AUBRYNN WHITTED

©2021 Aubrynn Whitted. All rights reserved.

PSALM 13
a psalm of David

How long, O Lord? Will you forget me forever?
    How long will you hide your face from me?
How long must I take counsel in my soul
    and have sorrow in my heart all the day?
How long shall my enemy be exalted over me?

Consider and answer me, O Lord my God;
    light up my eyes, lest I sleep the sleep of death,
lest my enemy say, "I have prevailed over him,"
    lest my foes rejoice because I am shaken.

But I have trusted in your steadfast love;
    my heart shall rejoice in your salvation.
I will sing to the Lord,
    because he has dealt bountifully with me.

CONTENTS

INTRODUCTION 7
Communion 9
Winter 10
Do Not Abandon 11
Faith Is Not Certainty 12
Why Have You Forsaken Me? 14
Courage, Dear Heart 15
Gracious Light 16
Too Good 17
On Christ the Solid Rock 18
Be Not Disconsolate 20
If You Should Mark Iniquities 21
Rest 22
In This Wounded World 23
Hit the Ground 24
Resurrection 26
Give Thanks 28
Fear Not, Little Flock 29
Rest Secure 30
The Sky is Ever Darkening 32
The Day Begins Anew 33
Why, Oh Lord, Why? 34
Who Can Ascend the Hill? 36

Not in Vain	37
Prayer	38
Willing and Able	40
Give Me Jesus	41
A Sonnet for the Doubting	42
What Can Save Me?	43
Doubting Heart	44
This Promise	45
A Sonnet of the Crucifixion	46
Christ, What Mighty Love	47
My Salvation	48
Oh Lord, How Often	49
By the Hand of Grace	50
This God	52
The Lord's Supper	54

INTRODUCTION

As Christians, we don't often talk about doubt. Sometimes we overcomplicate it or exclude it to a certain group of strugglers. We like quick and easy answers, yet they seldom resolve doubts. However, doubt is not the opposite of faith. In Mark chapter 9, it is faith that enables the father to express his doubt: "I believe; help my unbelief!"

Doubt is a part of the Christian life in a fallen world with fallen hearts, minds, and bodies. God himself recognizes this, including a whole book of poems and prayers in Scripture that express the depth and breadth of the human experience, a large part of which includes doubt.

Contrary to how we might treat ourselves or even others, the Lord does not admonish our doubts, belittle our fears, or scorn our weakness. Instead, through the Psalms he gives us the very words to speak to him, showing us how to be honest, to bring the doubts we all hide out into the open, and to flee for refuge under his wing, even when the uncertainty doesn't find its resolution.

These poems are lament prayers—they do not represent every facet of the human experience, but they resonate with many of mine. I wrote them to express my doubts, wrestle with the Lord, and preach to my own soul. I hope you find solace in these poems, knowing that faith and doubt can coexist. I hope you find grace in these poems, knowing Christ is kinder and more merciful than we could ever imagine.

Aubrynn Whitted

Communion

Why do you step aside
Or let this meal pass you by?
Not the worthy but the needy
Find their rest in Christ.

Come and take this cup,
Drink each blood-stained drop.
Take and chew this bread of life
And let it fill you up.

Come and know this truth,
Let it comfort you.
Come as sinners, poor and weak,
And find his mercies new.

Why do you hesitate?
Come now and partake.
You can trust he who prepared
This meal we could not make.

Winter

At dawn I wake; the air is dry and still.
The land is veiled with frost and with despair.
No flake of snow falls to redeem the chill
On this dull country, dreary, bleak, and bare.
The seeds are sown but lie dead in the ground,
Their blossoms thriving just in memory.
No sign of green or fruit here can be found;
It seems all earth has lost its energy.

In every season faithfulness is proved.
Every day the sun will rise; that's sure.
Whether hidden, by fog or cloud diffused,
Its light will shine, if we can feel its warmth
Or not. There is evidence in all things
That grace is rich and lavish and living,
No less because of this present pain
And no weaker in spite of this waiting.

Do Not Abandon
based on "A Prayer Against Evil Thoughts" by Thomas à Kempis

My God, do not abandon me!
For many thoughts assail me.
My faith falls to uncertainty,
All words of reason fail me.

These thoughts will not abandon me;
They batter, bruise, and bind me.
Where in this storm is mercy?
Where are you when they plague me?

How shall I pass through them unhurt?
You say you go before me.
What if this chaos finds no calm?
You say that you are with me.

Faith Is Not Certainty

Faith is not certainty.

Sometimes,
Faith is stumbling through the night,
    eyes trying, straining, failing to make out your shape ahead.

Faith is stepping forward, weak and weary,
    because all other directions are blocked.

Faith is following the worn trail through the shadowed woods
    though I cannot see the sky or sun.

Faith is hot coals on my feet,
    bloodied and bruised.

Faith is a smoldering hope when certainty's flames have died
    because the only other option is total despair.

Faith is leaping off the ladder,
    sink or swim.

Faith is grabbing the withering branch
    when the alternative is plummeting off the cliff.

Faith is a faint thought that you go before me,
    though none of my senses bear you witness.

Faith is crying out to the thick, dark clouds
    that might mask our Maker's smiling heart.

Faith is a weak call,
    a doubt-crippled prayer,
    a darkness-drenched plea for rescue:

I believe; help my unbelief!

Why Have You Forsaken Me?
based on Psalms 22 & 23

Oh why, my God, have you forsaken me?
I lift my eyes but see your hand not reach
To bring me sweet relief. My voice is spent
From crying out, yet Lord, your silence stings.

Oh you, who took me from the womb you made,
Why does deliverance seem so far away?
They say some cry to you and find relief,
But all I taste is bitter wine, dry toast.

Oh, be not far! For trouble lurks and none
Shall help but you. For you have hidden not
Your face, withdrawn your hand, nor stopped your ears.
But I can't keep myself from losing heart.

Oh Shepherd, may I walk with you again
In pastures green by waters still, and rest.

Courage, Dear Heart

Courage, dear heart.
Your tears are not forever.
The days of your sorrow
are just a little while,
though it doesn't feel like a little while.

I could offer you cliché words,
hollow phrases tied with a bow,
but all I have is questions of my own.

Why? I do not know.
How long? I couldn't guess.

Has our God forgotten us?
Has he turned a blind eye
to our abounding pain?
Has he shut up his ears
to our desperate cries?

How could he forget his beloved children?
Would he have moved heaven and earth
to save our souls
only to let us go?

No.

I am sure of this, if nothing else:
no matter what, he will not let us go.
His steadfast love for us will never fail.

Gracious Light

It seems dread is all I've known,
a sense of coming doom.
Is God good? Does he love me?
Will he comfort? Will he crush me?
Will his anger never turn?
Will his smile never burst
these clouds of doubt, to shine on me?

O gracious light,
you are real despite the clouds,
good despite this present darkness.
Though I walk in the valley of shadow,
the dark looming ever larger in my sight,
your goodness and mercy will follow me
all the days of my life.

Too Good

There is a love that causes this world
to pulse with beauty,
a steady rhythm making
this world beat.

It is hard to comprehend and
difficult to understand
when, looking through the lens of our pain,
this seems to be less of a lovely world
and more of a dark, desperate place.

It sounds too good to be true,
this proclamation of a steady hand
holding this world in orbit,
causing the sun to rise on a world
so lost and worthy of utter darkness.
It is a testament to affection.
So while it may be too good
for us to understand it,
that doesn't change the fact
that it is
true.

On Christ the Solid Rock

"On Christ the solid rock I stand"
I sing, but doubt and stumble.
I do not know if I am held by you,
and so I do not know if I am safely hidden,
fixed on that firm foundation.
Am I seated on the sinking sand?
When the floods rise
and winds begin to whip and lash,
will I be safe? Or will I fall and sink
and drown, body worn down beneath the weight?

On Christ the solid rock I stand—
what if I cannot stand?
Can I fall on you, faith faltering,
and find a refuge from this sinking sand?
I cannot make myself believe
or give myself a sweet relief some will say they feel.
I cannot make myself stand—
but can it be
that you will hold me anyway?

Your solid rock amidst the sinking sand
does not require
two solid legs to stand strong and straight,
which do not quake or buckle;
it merely requires a resting,
a giving up of reliance on self-strength,
even a falling upon your shore,
not out of reach of the winds of doubt or fear
but safe from all their threats and harm.

On Christ the solid rock I stand—
not because my legs are strong and never shake,
but because Christ is the solid rock.

Be Not Disconsolate

My soul, be not disconsolate, though grieved.
Your God, your help, has not forgotten you.
He sees your ways and knows your paths; he sleeps
And tarries not; his eyes, not passive, watch.

My soul, say not you hope in vain—his strength
Shall hold you even when your own is spent.
His hands now scarred, once wounded, work his will.
Your God who chose you shall not let you go.

Our help, he holds us steady with his hand.
My God has not—shall not—cast out his own.
My Shepherd gathers in his arms his sheep
To keep them all their days according to

His promise. Oh my soul, do not forsake
Your comfort—he has not forsaken you.

If You Should Mark Iniquities

If you should mark iniquities, oh Lord,
Then who could stand? For man is frail and faint.
What other hope could hold us, tired and sore?
And who could hold our sin, its heavy weight?
Your work alone—your sweat, your blood, not mine—
Has born this load and shouldered grief so strong.
With you, there is forgiveness, who inclines
To hear us, when we lift complaint or song.
To whom then shall I flee, or throw my life
Upon? Who's steadfast, faithful, true, and good?
Lord, I have nowhere else to flee. If Christ
Marks not iniquities, nor counts our sin,
Then this I know: that though I fear and fall
And fail, then fret, my Lord has paid it all.

Rest

I am tired, broken down, and weary.
All these years, and only variations
on the same old themes, same fears.

Yet why do I hesitate
to truly come and lay down my head?

For you have said:

Come to me, all who are weary,
and I will give you more work.

No—come to me, all who are weary,
and I will add to your burden.

No—come to me, all who are weary,
and I will increase your guilt
and compound your shame; I'll
wait until you fully appreciate
all I went through before blessing
you, before forgiving; only after
you get your prayers in shape,
your repentance right, your faith less
wobbly and weak. And maybe then—

No. You have said:

Come to me, all who are weary,
and I will give you
rest.

In This Wounded World

Grace displayed for weary sinners
through the wounds of the Lord.
In his blood and in his tears,
love portrayed to all the world.

What other God would immerse himself in our sorrows?
What other God give all of himself for his people?

You have proved the heights you will go to
in saving your suffering sinners
to make us saints in your name,
for our joy and for your own sake.

No other God would wrap himself in human flesh.
No other God would shoulder our sorrows and griefs.

In this wounded world you died,
not for our deserving or your need,
but all a plain bounty of love
poured out onto each one of us.

Hit the Ground

You hit the ground
hard.

Your face,
once
bright
And beautiful,
now streaked with sorrow.
Your heart,
once light
and loving,
now languishing.
You thought you'd feel
his arms
holding you close,
keeping you up;
but instead you feel
the impact
as your legs give way,
your strength gives up,
and you fall.

His arms never lifted,
never left your side.
Your sorrow speaks
louder than truth,
sometimes,
when it has turned
to despair.

But despair is not truth.
Despair doesn't recognize
his presence.
Despair doesn't trust
his intentions.
Despair doesn't acknowledge
his affection.

You are held
forever.

Resurrection
for Levi

Dirt is dug up
and a casket is laid
in the cold, hard ground.

While family stands by,
loved ones and friends,
to see their beloved, breathless.

We speak of joy after sorrow,
but the morning only brings pain,
and it's hard to have hope for tomorrow.

How can we look up
when our world is crumbling?
How can we believe he is love?

The night can't last always.
Even when it seems to drag on and on,
it must break into dawn.

Praise him that the grave is not the end,
that though death and sorrow linger,
they don't have the final say.

I believe you are the resurrection and the life,
but help my unbelief.
I believe you are love,
I believe you are good,
but help my unbelief.

When a grave is filled with a loved one
and a home is left too empty,
it's hard to find the heart to rejoice.

Help my unbelief when
the aches and cries of the ones left behind
are filled with such sorrow and grief.

I love him, but I don't understand,
and to trust, I have to fight.
I believe, but help my unbelief;

you are the resurrection and the life.

Give Thanks

Gazing at the sorrow and the brokenness
makes me question what I know is true,
makes me wonder whether your love is as you've promised.
Looking at this world,
it seems you're nowhere to be found,
for the sorrow seems so much stronger
and my doubt grows deeper.

Where is my God
in the midst of this turmoil?

Christ's love—not always tangible or perceived—
is nevertheless constant and consuming,
relentlessly poured upon me.
Through each step of this winding, jarring path,
his mercies are new, and sufficient.

When the season of giving thanks comes to pass
and my heart is finding it hard to give thanks,
and the gray sky is looming,
I'll look around.
May the love you have be evident
in the bounty of food, of friendship, and
blessings upon blessings poured out,
despite all the pain.
Through all you've done,
your steadfast love follows me,
and I give thanks.

Fear Not, Little Flock

I try to cover up my thoughts,
or convert them into better ones,
change them altogether
into something I'm not ashamed of.

But doesn't he know them already?
Would he be surprised if I brought them,
honest and raw, to him?
Would he not desire me to do so?

Do I think anything I do
can impede his plans for me
or cause me to slip from his grasp?
How can they do any such thing?
For he is not ashamed of me.

Fear not, little flock—
has he not told us this truth?
He is pleased, not begrudged, to love us,
and willing even to give us the kingdom.

Rest Secure

Last night I heard thunder
roar across the sky,
and I must confess:
I've never felt so aware of your wrath
as I felt that night,
and never so small beneath your might
as then.
I heard the house creak
and the trees sway
beneath the power,
and I felt my insignificance
and my weakness.

This God can bend the trees in half,
can crush this house beneath his weight,
can cause the winds to strike me
and the lightning to destroy me,
and would be perfectly justified in doing so—
but this God chooses mercy,
compassion, and grace.

After the storm comes the calm,
like a sweet breath of air;
and I know your love is stronger
than I have ever seen before,
for the same One who lit the lightning
and cracked the thunder
is the same One who wrapped himself in human flesh
and came upon this earth to suffer
and die beneath all the weight

of that wrath and that might
so that I might rest secure,
so I might not feel the terror of the night
nor fear the powerful hand of God,
because his is also a gentle hand of grace;
and in all of his immense power,
holiness, and beauty,
he still cares for me.

The Sky is Ever Darkening

The sky is ever darkening in hue.
The night is all round quiet, still, and blue.
The faintest streams of light the moon alone
Casts o'er the earth; the stars have hardly shone.
Evading rest, eluding peace, and fear
And heavy melancholy linger here.
Exhaustion finds me lying in my bed,
And though the night is still, I cannot rest.

But soon, the shades of night will quickly fly
When dawn's light steals across the darkened sky.
The dusky hues of night will fade from sight
Before the sun and morning's amber light.
Perhaps then, rest will bid my mind and fears to calm
And I'll finally believe I was held
all along.

The Day Begins Anew

The day begins anew, and Lord,
I pray you keep my eyes on you.
That everything I do be done
In grace and mercy, love and truth.
That I'd be quick to serve with love—
Not of guilt or cold compulsion—
And trust my works are not enough
To determine my salvation.
Your righteousness, so pure, made mine!
I don't deserve such wondrous grace.
This day, may hope rest not on me,
But may I trust and seek your face.
Yet when I stumble, Lord I pray—
I know you'll hold me fast always.

Why, Oh Lord, Why?

Why, oh Lord, why?

Why do you let the orphans prosper
but cast suffering on your sons?
Where are you in this mess,
when all around is chaos?

Do you—who holds the earth,
who directs the stars,
who plans each course—
stand far away? Do you stand stoic in the sky
while those you love weep alone,
discarded and forgotten?
My questions rise to meet you,
but do they dissolve before they reach you?

Silence.

Who is wise
in all the earth?

Have I formed the mountain slopes
or held the oceans in my hands?
Has my knowledge reached on high
that I should discern your thoughts?
My questions dissolve before you.

You hold me when the sun is warm upon my face,
and when the sky is gray.
You give and take away,

not according to whims
but sovereign plans.
You weep with us, rejoice with us,
your heart towards us is full of love.
You hold us always.

This pain has a purpose I can't see—
but that alone could never comfort me.

My questions reach your ear and
find your heart,
even when no answers run to meet me.
My own tears are a drop to your ocean.
The breaking in my heart
is joy to your lament.

You are wise, oh Lord;
and you are near.
That
is answer enough.

Who Can Ascend the Hill?
based on Psalm 24

I cannot ascend the hill of the Lord,
but Christ shouldered his cross and climbed to Calvary.
I cannot stand in his holy place,
but Christ enters his presence with a plea on my behalf.
My hands are bloodied, my heart impure,
but Christ knew no deceit, no false words.
Yet this blessing received from the Lord
is poured upon us, and righteousness
bestowed on us,
and salvation from the Lord.

Not in Vain

Do you think that he has let you slip
out of his mind, like chaff?
It seems his promises are slow,
that you're no more than a passing thought.

But if Christ suffered as a man
for the joy set before him,
and rose again and broke death's sting,
then maybe grief is not in vain.

And he who bore such sin and wrath
all for our sakes, how could he leave?
He won't so quickly leave his sons,
nor forsake his flock of sheep.

His promises can never come untrue;
his faithfulness is as sure as his strong grasp.

Oh my soul, he has not forgotten you.

Prayer

Sometimes,
I cannot pray.
Can I stir within myself
a desire to pour out my heart
to a God for whom I hold so many doubts?
Every effort proves fallen,
every word seems fake and flat.
I wonder if I even have
the faith to believe that you hear.

Do you truly hear?
Surely; invariably.
But why do you hear?
Do you listen to hear our angelic voices,
listing our progress and proving ourselves?
To see just how much love we have,
to reward us for our excellent faith?
Hardly.
Yet neither do you stop up your ears,
turn a blind eye, or refuse to listen
when we pour our hearts out to you.

You listen to our prayers—could this be true?—
because you love us, and we are covered
wholly in Christ's blood.
You do not decide to be merciful
only after hearing our prayers—
indeed, could we even find the heart to pray
if not moved by your preexisting mercy?

You hear each prayer because
you are the God who hears,
and because you are gracious and merciful.

Willing and Able

Jesus, if you are willing,
if you can hear me,
won't you save me,
won't you be near me?

Jesus, if you are able,
why don't you reach down,
illuminate this dark,
and show your power now?

Jesus, if you are near me,
won't you demonstrate
this truth, if you
abound in grace?

Jesus, if you are even here at all—

In my inability to do much of anything,
you have given me grace to cry out,
"I believe; help my unbelief."

That is evidence you are near,
and you are willing and able.

Give Me Jesus

If you never give me perfect faith
or never take this doubt away,
just give me Jesus.

If I never see the sun this life
but darkness, and just know this strife,
just give me Jesus.

If my tears will never cease to flow
while I walk this earth below,
just give me Jesus.

If every joy is laced with pain
and every deed shadowed by shame,
just give me Jesus.

When emotions seem so strong
I can't discern what's right or wrong,
just give me Jesus.

If the questions never feel resolved
and worry never is dissolved,
just give me Jesus.

When I rise or when I fall,
in every moment, through it all,
just give me Jesus.

A Sonnet for the Doubting

Each time I take my eyes off you, I doubt
And focus on and fear the wild wind's rage.
I sink and feel the waves seethe and surround.
My eyes, when gazing at the wind and waves,
Are not upon your steadfast loving face.
Despair in these hard times is all I know;
Its dismal, frightful snare, I can't escape.
Though full of sin and shame, upon the Lord
I cast my cares and fears, and lift my face.
My Savior's work upon the cross is done,
And that alone can me from this pit raise.
His grace can save my wretched soul, alone.
Lord, help my eyes not stray from your kind face,
And help me trust in nothing but your grace.

What Can Save Me?

What can save me or remake me?
What can hold me fast and sure?
What in heaven or earth can free me
From this fear that grips my soul?

Can the faith I try to stir up
Or the love I try to feel?
Can the depth of sorrow in me
Be a comfort in my fear?

Can my tears or can my pleading,
Can my thirst to have control?
Can the strength I find within me
Be a means to save my soul?

Can the words I say, my actions,
Deeds of good or kindness free?
Can an act of service soothe and
Silence each anxiety?

Can I add up hours spent praying,
Digging deep into Scripture?
Can a thousand poems save me,
Can these good pursuits preserve?

Christ alone has shown me mercy,
By his blood has proved his grace.
He who keeps me has redeemed me;
He shall never turn his face.

Doubting Heart

Oh doubting heart,
he does not condemn you.
Do you think that if you let him see
the doubts you hide within
that he will scoff, or seem surprised,
or give you punishment?

Does he not know our wavering hearts,
so prone to doubt and fear?
He does not let salvation rest
on our resolve to keep it,
nor will he let his promise bend
according to our weakness.

So what have we amidst the pain
and in the storms of unbelief,
when faith seems taut and thin?
We have this hope, this confidence,
this anchor sure and steady:
Christ has gone in, in our place,
and lives to save and keep us.

This Promise

I don't believe you are enough for me
Or trust in your unending grace.
I don't believe in kind-hearted mercy
Or a love strong enough to save.

I say I believe in your saving grace,
Your finished work, your covenant;
But if I lived out this truth every day,
I would not fear your rejection.

I talk the talk and believe in my head,
But my heart, it is in discord.
I want to believe, I want to depend;
Lord, help me to trust in your Word.

You've said, "Confess and I will forgive you
And cleanse you from unrighteousness."
So may I hold fast to this constant truth,
This gift, this love, and this promise.

A Sonnet of the Crucifixion

Lord Jesus, Son of God you are, and yet,
As man, you—humbled to the grave, our grave—
Become a lamb led to be killed. Blameless,
You take upon yourself the sin, the weight.
As cries ring out our gracious God to blame,
We, hardened, turn our backs on you, and you
Oh lamb of God, are whipped and bruised, then slain;
You're taken down and laid inside a tomb.
Is there a grief so deep as on that day
Where holy wrath and unmatched grace collide?
Where, though beloved and pure in every way,
He's cast down for us, his unfaithful bride.
The darkest day of deepest pain has shown
The deepest grace this world has ever known.

Christ, What Mighty Love

Christ, what mighty love has found our roving hearts,
What powerful blood has bought and held our souls,
That even when we wander, as we're prone,
We are not lost—we never leave your grasp.

Christ, what mighty love has our affection sealed,
What holy grace has many sins revealed,
And all those sins forgiven and made clean;
We're reconciled to God through Christ.

Christ, what mighty love our anxious fear has put
To rest, and does each day repeatedly,
Assuring us of grace deeper than sin,
Both in despair and when we're full of pride.

Christ, what mighty love has brought to us
The grief and suffering of yourself.
Great comfort amidst sorrow, Christ, you are;
How sweet the friendship of the Lord to us.

Christ, what mighty love has calmed our fear that yours
Is like our love: forgetful, faithless, blind.
What mighty love has stilled our ceaseless strife,
What mighty love has found us where we are.

My Salvation

If I am prone to wander, Christ is quick to pardon.
If I am quick to anger, Christ is full of patience.
If I am full of sin, Christ abounds in grace.
If I abound in doubt, Christ does not condemn me.
If I am self-condemning, Christ still loves and holds me.
If I am apt to fall, Christ has never left me.
If I tend toward distraction, Christ does not forget me.
If I am lacking faith, Christ does not lack mercy.
If I'm inclined to fear, Christ is void of harshness.
If I am void of love, Christ is my salvation.

Though I am all these things, and more,
nothing depends on me;
for if I'm void of all else, still,
Christ is my salvation.

Oh Lord, How Often

Oh Lord, how often I forget you.
How frequently my thoughts will shift
and battle, my trust ebb and flow.
Desire turns to begrudging duty
and beauty pales to lifeless gray.

If I could lose my salvation, I would!
For what's to keep me from falling?
How could I keep what I could not make?
No; Lord, you must hold me!
I am inadequate; if left up to me,
I'd lose it, I'd forget it, I'd just walk away.

But Lord, you hold me fast.
When my heart is not in it,
my gut to ignore, prone to wander,
you are faithful still.
I would not still be in the fight—
I'd have quit it long ago—
if not for you to lead me on,
to call me, shape me, save me.

By the Hand of Grace

All fruit seems to be invisible to
the one from whom it grows.
But that fruit is not his,
and he cannot make it;
so how well can he see it?

He did not plant the roots.
He does not water them,
causing their growth;
and so how can he know
by searching inward
whether that tree bears fruit?

How can he know
without another observer?
How can he look
objectively at his heart
without being driven to despair?

No one can watch fruit visibly grow,
but one can see its finished product.
In the midst of waiting, growth seems slow,
but the product shows it is steady and sure.

This is a strange, wonderful paradox:
the growing awareness of one's own deadness
is a great indicator of the growth in one's fruit.

It is probable that when the fruit
one bears is unseen, unknown to them,
there are roots beneath the surface,
growing by the tender hand of grace.

This God

Who is this God who rules this world?
My circumstances would have me say:

A Father who prepares the feast
And lets us eat, begrudgingly.
Who sees our griefs and knows our woes
And tells us we could have it worse.
Who shakes his head each time we fall;
Who lifts us up, but lets us go.
Who saves us from all death and hell
To leave us in this fight alone.
Whose grace is real but lacking strength,
Whose justice, above all else, reigns.
Whose heart is quick in showing wrath
But stingy in bestowing grace.

This is not the God who lives—
Who is this God who made my soul?

The Shepherd who became the sheep
And leads us to this feast he's made.
Who calls the wayward child home
And runs to see him, to embrace.
Who endured wrath and suffered wounds
To bring his people sweet relief.
Who bore our sorrows on himself
And never minimizes grief.
Who lifts us every time we slip
And never weakens his firm grip.

Who walks beside us, leading us,
And never shames or condemns us.
Whose grace is greater than all sin,
Whose kindness can't be discouraged.
Whose patience for us won't wear thin,
Whose mercies are new each moment.

The Lord's Supper

The table is laden with a meal.
Words are spoken of invitation,
of welcome, of mercy;
and yet,
I feel too far to receive it.

This is a meal to be shared
by brothers and sisters,
the body of Christ,
a communal affair;
and yet,
I feel so disconnected.

Can I touch my lips to this bread
or taste this sweet juice upon my tongue?
This meal is not deserved of me;
and yet,
that very reality drives me to partake.

This bite of bread and sip of wine
is a mercy to me.
With very little faith
the whole Christ I receive.

This meal is a tangible reminder
of what I need to remember every moment,
a palpable thing to weaken my doubts
of his love;
for his blood is as real as the cup that I hold,
and this bread, as real as the body he broke.

He doesn't show us our sin
to leave us in shame,
but to bring us to the table
and invite us to partake.
A welcome still standing:
come, eat and drink.

CPSIA information can be obtained
at www.ICGtesting.com
Printed in the USA
BVHW041115110821
614094BV00012B/1260